Δ

THE DELTA INITIATIVE

How to Easily, Permanently Change Whatever Sucks In Your Business Or Your Life, in 30 Minutes a day, in 120 Days or Less

©2005 JIM ACKERMAN

All rights reserved. This book, and the accompanying audio and software programs, may not be reproduced in whole or in part, or transmitted in any form, or by any means electronic, mechanical, photocopying, recording, or other, without written permission from the publisher, except by a reviewer who may quote brief passages in a review.

Excerpts are permitted for editorial purposes, with advance notice to publisher, as long as an author's credit is included and the author is provided with copies. Contact Ascend Marketing, Inc. at 801.254.7964 for specific required credit language.

Ackerman, Jim
The Delta Initiative: How to Easily, Permanently Change Whatever Sucks In Your Business Or Your Life, in 30 Minutes a day, in 120 Days or Less

ISBN: 1-59971-210-5

Published in cooperation with Aardvark Publishing Co.
by Ascend Publishing
Subsidiary of Ascend Marketing, Inc.
1044 Louise Meadow Dr
South Jordan UT 84095
801.254.7964
www.ascendmarketing.com
www.thedeltainitiative.com

CONTENTS

INTRODUCTION – NEVER MIND, MAYBE

CHAPTER 1
THE CASE FOR CHANGE

CHAPTER 2
THE 5 U-NEEDS

CHAPTER 3
WHAT TO DOS

CHAPTER 4
HOW TO DO ITS

CHAPTER 5
RESOURCES TO GET IT DONE

CHAPTER 6
FEEDBACK TO MAKE SURE YOU DO IT RIGHT

CHAPTER 7
ACCOUNTABILITY TO MAKE SURE YOU ACTUALLY DO IT

CHAPTER 8
BACKTIME ACTION PLAN

CONCLUSION

About the Author
Tools

ACKNOWLEDGEMENTS

I must acknowledge, thank, and express my love to my wife, Susan, who personifies the quest for constant and never-ending improvement for herself and her family.

Also to my nine children, their spouses and my grandchildren. It is more for them than for myself that I strive to be a better man.

I am grateful for my departed parents who taught me that if I work hard, I can accomplish anything to which I set my mind. Even changing things about me that I don't like.

Long overdue is acknowledgement to Mrs. Hummer, my fifth grade teacher, whose constant pounding on the principles of grammar has served me throughout my life. How I hated diagramming all those sentences. How I bless her for it now. Mrs. Hummer, wherever you are, I'm sure this isn't perfect, but I pray it will do.

Finally, to Tiffany Berg, who created her book, *Take Courage, A Message Of Hope After Hurricane Katrina,* and had it published just two weeks after that monumental disaster stuck. She showed me it can be done. Thanks to her as well for the excellent cover design.

∆ INTRODUCTION ∆
Never Mind, maybe

Look, this may be a waste of time for both of us.

Fact is, less than 10% of the books that get sold, get read. Of people who buy self-improvement books, listen to audio programs or attend conferences, conventions, seminars and workshops, implementation rates are between 1.4 and 8.4 percent.

And to be perfectly honest with you, even though I *know* the stuff I'm about to share with you, I'm no poster child for implementation. I've helped hundreds of others change, and I've had my own successes along the way, but I know more than I do. That doesn't make me unique among the gurus of any discipline, by the way. I just want you to know, up front, I'm nothing special. That, of course, should give you hope. If I can use this stuff, you should certainly be able to use it too.

Nevertheless, the odds are you're not going to change anything, with or without this book. And if this is just a leisurely, nice to know romp for you, well it's up to you of course, but if it were me, I'd rather watch a ballgame.

I'm not trying to talk you out of anything, I'm just being realistic, which is what you have to be if you really expect to change.

On the other hand, some people *do* change. Some people *have* to. A few *want* to, and have what it takes to productively change for the better on a consistent basis. Some people really want to change, and they really *can*, but they've never discovered how.

INTRODUCTION

Let's face it. Something isn't good in *your* life. Hey, if everything was hunky dorey, you wouldn't be reading this. And there isn't a human on the planet for whom something -- at least one thing -- isn't just right.

The Greek letter **Delta** is the scientific notation for change. All of us have at least one thing we're out to change about ourselves or our businesses or our lives. That's our quest. That's our **"Delta Initiative."**

The cool part is, change isn't anywhere near as difficult as everybody makes it out to be.

You *can* teach an old dog new tricks, and you can do it quickly, with permanent results. That's what *The Delta Initiative* is all about. From quitting smoking to renewing your marriage, from losing 10 pounds to making 10 million bucks. Whatever your quest, following the simple formula I'm about to reveal will change your business and/or your life, in 120 days or less.

If you do decide to go on from here, I have some suggestions...

Read the entire book through once. It'll only take you an hour or so.

Next, listen to the CD at least once, but preferably several times. Its a good idea to "pound these ideas into your brain."

Then decide if you really are going to DO anything about it. If so, read the book a second time with pen and notebook in hand, writing your observations along the way. This may not be a one-sitting read.

The third time through is the charm. Use the **30-Minute Backtimed Action Plan Template** I've included on the same CD as the audio program, and complete the action items. By now you will have selected what I call your **"Delta Initiative Target,"** and you'll be well on your way to making the change you really want to make in your life.

∆ 1 ∆
THE CASE FOR CHANGE

"I would find out what is wrong with me, and correct it. Then I might have a chance to profit by my mistakes and learn something from the experience of others..."

Napoleon Hill

The Case for Change

"If you always do what you've always done, you'll always get what you've always got."

I don't know who the first person to say that was, but it may be the most profound truth ever wrought in the history of mankind.

You can only reap what you sow, and if you continue to sow the same seeds, you can only harvest the same crop.

Now look, we've got to be honest with each other, and moreover, you've got to be honest with yourself. A lot of us *say* we want things to be different, but we're obviously lying to ourselves. We may *wish* things were different, but down deep, we really don't *want* them to be different. If we did, we'd do something about it. And we don't. What I'm saying is, 93% of us don't. At least not on a consistent enough basis to have the kind of lives we don't have to gripe and moan about all the time.

I'm not going to go into a rant about desire and the role it plays in the change process. You've heard that a million times. You know you need it, at least enough to make you take action.

But the truth is, you really don't need much desire to change if you follow The Delta Initiative formula.

A more important ingredient is *humility*. If you want to change, you're going to have to be humble enough to admit to yourself that your life, the way it is, isn't acceptable, and it's your own fault.

You're also going to have to admit that you may not be able to make the necessary changes all by yourself.

And finally, you're going to have to relinquish some control to somebody else, at least temporarily, if you're going to change things.

But I digress. I was making the case *for* change, not telling you *how* to change… yet.

The case for change is really quite simple.

Your life sucks!

At least some aspect or aspects of it.

No, I'm serious. You're reading this for a reason, aren't you?

Maybe you can't get your employees on the same page and it's bringing down, or holding back your company. That sucks! It sucks time, money, profits, morale and energy out of you and your company.

Maybe you and your spouse are just going through the motions. The spark has gone out, or is close to it. That can suck the life out of a family. It can suck you dry physically, mentally, emotionally, spiritually and financially. What could suck more than that?

Maybe you've been smoking since you were 12 and you're going to DIE!

Maybe you've been morbidly obese your whole life and you're going to DIE!

Maybe you've been told you're chronically depressed, or Adult ADD, or bi-polar or any number of other psychological disorders and you're going to DIE! (Or worse, kill somebody else!)

Maybe you're stuck in a dead-end, boring, get

The Case For Change

nowhere, do nothing job that is sucking the vitality and joy of life right out of you, and you're going to DIE!

Maybe you just need to get out of your excess consumer debt, and stay out.

Maybe your marketing is ineffective and your profits aren't what they ought to be.

Maybe the competition is killing you or maybe you sell a "me-too" product and your business is owning you instead of the other way around.

It ALL sucks, doesn't it?

Go ahead, say it… Say it loud… No, shout it loud…

THIS STUFF SUCKS!

Okay, doesn't that feel better now? It's on the table. And that's the case for change.

Something sucks and you don't want it to any more.

Wait a minute. Which is it? You don't *want* it to suck any more, or you *wish* it wouldn't suck any more?

Big difference. And here's how you know whether you're a *wanter* or a *wisher*…

Are you willing to spend 30 minutes a day for the next 120 days to change it?

Are you? That all it's likely to take.

If you're willing to make that investment, you probably *want* it to change. If not, you're only *wishing* and you should go back to the ballgame.

If you make the decision to turn the page, I'll assume you're a stop-the-sucking person and we go on. If you don't, enjoy the ballgame.

The Case For Change

Oh, one more thing. I'm not promising you'll have 10 million bucks in 120 days, or that you'll lose 100 pounds in four months. I'm not promising the fire will be all the way back in your marriage or that your entire psychosis will be cured by then. (I'm also not saying it won't.)

What I am saying is, by applying The Delta Initiative formula, you will have changed the way you go about the things that make your life suck. When you change those things, you are sowing new seeds. And when you sow new seeds, you WILL reap a new harvest.

When you no longer do what you've always done, you can no longer get what you've always got.

YOUR ACTION ITEMS...

☛ Identify just one thing that sucks in your life that you want to change. Again, I mean really *want* to change. In other words, what do you want to change badly enough that you're willing to spend a minimum of 30 minutes a day working on that change, for the next 120 days?

☛ Write it down on paper. Then write out in detail all the things about this aspect of your life that is costing you. I'm talking about all the implications of this thing. Physical, emotional, mental, spiritual, financial, relationship. I want you to be perfectly clear and honest on how bad it really is. I want you to feel all the exquisite pain it's causing you and why you know this thing MUST change.

☛ Finally, write out in as much detail as possible, all the glorious implications of making the change. What will life be like when this

THE CASE FOR CHANGE

aspect of your life has changed? Again, what will be the exquisite physical, emotional, mental, spiritual, financial and relationship benefits of the change?

Be detailed, but don't force it. If you don't anticipate financial benefits, for example, don't feel like you have to invent them. But don't skip over any category of benefits too lightly either.

And remember, just pick one thing. We will eat those "sucky elephants" that are tormenting your life, one bite at a time, in 30 minute, 120 day chunks.

∆ 2 ∆
INTRODUCING THE 5 U-NEEDS

"They say that time changes things, but you actually have to change them yourself."

Andy Warhol

INTRODUCING THE 5 U-NEEDS

The *Delta Initiative* is based on the simple premise that there are five things you need – I call them "U-needs" – if you are to effectively initiate change in any aspect of your life.

I will introduce them all here, then we'll discuss them in detail in subsequent chapters.

If you are to succeed at the highest levels, you need these five key elements...

1. **The "What-To-Dos"** – You simply must know what to do.

2. **The "How-To-Do-Its"** – How you do the whats can have an exponential impact on the results you get. A two-word change in a headline, for example, can increase response to an ad by 1,000%.

3. **Resources to get it done** – nobody can do it all alone. You need resources. Books, tapes and events may be resources for *telling* you some of the whats and hows, but they can't help you actually get things done.

4. **Feedback to make sure you do it right** – One of the biggest reasons people don't take action following reading books, listening to tapes or attending events, is fear of failure; fear of doing it wrong. Feedback gives you the confidence to know you can do it right.

5. **Accountability to make sure you actually do it** – Somebody has to hold your feet to the fire. Somebody has to consistently hold you accountable to make sure you do what you know you should, in a timely fashion.

INTRODUCING THE 5 U-NEEDS

YOUR ACTION ITEMS...

☛ STOP NOW and do the action items from Chapter 1. Who you kidding? No more cheating! Then on to this Chapter's work.

☛ Evaluate your assets. Write out which of these five U-needs you think you currently have in place, if any, in your quest to change the thing you've identified as your first *"Delta Initiative target."*

☛ Assign a preliminary value on a scale of 1 to 5 - with one being ready to rock and roll and five being between a rock and a hard place - where you stand with each of the U-needs in terms of readiness to proceed with your 30 minutes a day for 120 days. (This is only preliminary of course, because you haven't read the rest of the book yet.)

☛ Write out what you may need to do to get the rest of the U-needs in place so you can proceed with your change project.

▲ 3 ▲

U-NEED #1
THE WHAT-TO-DOS

"...our finest moments are most likely to occur when we are feeling deeply uncomfortable, unhappy, or unfilfilled. For it is only in such moments, propelled by our discomfort, that we are likely to step out of our ruts and start searching for different ways or truer answers."

M. Scott Peck

The What-To-Dos

You simply must know what to do.

Frankly, while this isn't necessarily a slam dunk, it is the easiest part of the formula.

This is the stuff you get from books, audio programs, and seminars.

Is there any shortage of information on how to stop smoking, lose weight, repair your relationships or make a fortune?

Heck no! And most of the how-to information out there is good information. I mean, it's valid.

But this is your first gut check. Are you willing to go find the information?

I spend most of my time helping small and mid-size businesses **get more customers and get more money out of the ones they've already got**. I do this by helping them change their sales, marketing and advertising systems to generate dramatically better results.

The thing that amazes me most, though, is not that most of these business people don't have a clue about the what-to-dos in their marketing. The thing that blows me away is that, until they hook up with me, they do nothing to find out!

And they wonder why their marketing sucks!

There are about a gazillion books out there on how to market your small business.

People go to college to learn how to do this marketing and advertising stuff.

The What-To-Dos

Yes, the information abounds. You can pay a little for it by buying books from little-known authors, or your can attend $5,000.00 weekend bootcamps by the likes of Anthony Robbins and Jay Abraham.

Believe me, these guys are good, and worth the money. I've paid to attend these kinds of events and I've spoken at them as well. I've even put on a few of my own.

So the information… the What-to-dos… is out there. But it ain't going to just automatically show up at your door. You gotta be on the lookout for it. You have to go in search of it. And the truth is, most of the time, you're going to have to be willing to pay for it. A little or a lot, it's still going to cost you some money.

More importantly, it will cost you time. You have to take the time to find the information, and then you have to assimilate it.

Another challenge with the what-to-dos is knowing which what-do-dos are right for you.

Your yellow-page rep, Anthony Robbins, your therapist, Dr. Phil, *ME*... we'll all tell you what to do. But sometimes there's a conflict or contradiction in the advice you get.

For example, one of the great myths about advertising, eternally propagated by media reps and ad agency types alike, is that your ad must be seen or heard seven times before it makes an impression.

Bull!

We know, from the world of direct response marketing, that one exposure to your ad is enough, if it's the right ad, to the right people.

My point is, if the wrong person is giving you the wrong what-to-dos, you can waste a lot of time and money and get a very bad result.

The What-To-Dos

So, here are some tips for finding the right what-to-dos.

1. Consider your specific situation. Are your needs the same as others who are being advised by any given source of what-to-dos? If so, the what-to-dos offered by the source are probably useful. Remember, small business is a lot different from big business. What works for GM or GE may be a disaster for Mom & Pop.

2. Consider the source. What are their qualifications? Where do they get their information? And perhaps most importantly, what are their motivations? If a media rep or ad agency tells you to run a longer ad schedule, consider their motivation for making that recommendation. Could it be they get paid on commission, so the more you spend, the more they make?

3. Check track record. If the what-to-dos actually work for others, there's a good chance

they'll work for you, if you implement correctly (the how-to-do-its). Naturally, again, the "others" must be others who are like you.

4. Be selective. You can't do it all, so don't try. As you accumulate sources for your what-to-dos, run them through your own personal BS detector. Look at all comers with a critical eye and select your actions based on your thoughtful analysis. Play devil's advocate with yourself. Even if an action looks, sounds and feels good on the surface, try to find the holes in it before you adopt.

5. Don't get so carried away with number 4 above that you suffer the "paralysis of analysis." Remember change requires more than just thinking. You have to *DO* something.

THE WHAT-TO-DOS

YOUR ACTION ITEMS...

☛ Do a Google Search for information about how to change whatever you have identified as your "Delta Initiative target."

☛ Identify books, programs, articles and other sources of information about the change you want to make.

☛ Begin to gather and evaluate, and begin to develop a philosophy about what you are going to do to affect the desired changes in your life.

☛ Write down both the sources and your reactions to them as you evaluate each.

These assignments may take some time, so do them in as many 30-minute chunks as it takes.

∆ 4 ∆
U-NEED #2
THE HOW-TO-DO-ITS

"I am always doing that which I can not do, in order that I may learn how to do it."

Pablo Picasso

4

How you *do* the *whats* can have an exponential impact on the results you get. I once changed two words in a headline and increased results from five or six responses per time it ran to 50 or 60. That's a 1,000% increase!

Important point. Most of the books and programs you find out there that begin with the words "How To" should really begin with the words "What To".

Most how-to books, audio programs and seminars are heavy on the what-to-dos, but light on the how-to-do-its. Not all, but most.

Unfortunately, it's tough to come by the specific, step-by-step how-tos of just about anything.

This isn't always the fault of the authors and speakers who put these materials together. After all, execution of almost anything has to be done on an individual basis.

Look at me and this book. How can I give you the specific how-to-do-its for your change quest? I don't know what you're trying to change. Now, I've included some specific assignments, but aren't those really what-to-do things?

I said, "Do a Google search," for example. I didn't say, "Enter www.google.com on your web browser.

"In the search box type in the word…"

In other words I leave it to you to figure out most of the how-to-do-its. You have to determine what your Delta Initiative target is, then you have to do the Google thing, then you have to read and evaluate, then do the writing part of the assignment.

And think how easy a Google search is. Imagine something as complex as how to write a good headline for your ad. Why, to do that you need to know your Unique Purchase Appeal, all the features and benefits of your product or service, what the offer is, all the possible headline styles, and on and on it goes.

And writing a good headline for an ad may be duck soup compared to finding a new way to show your love for your spouse. How does anybody step-by-step that one?

So, not all the fault lies with the writers and speakers who provide the information, although I do believe that they shoulder some of the burden of responsibility. It is difficult to provide meaningful how-to-do-its. It's not impossible.

Step by step procedures, analytical processes, methods, techniques, even nuances, can be communicated and demonstrated. That's how we teach skills. And skills are no more than the appropriate execution of the how-to-do-its.

Remember also that there is a difference between knowing what the how-to-do-its are and good execution of them. That is what skill is all about.

In that light, stamp the following two critical axioms on your frontal lobes...

1. Anything worth doing is worth doing... POORLY... at first.

I don't think any kid has ever walked to the plate and hit a home run, the very first time he picked up a baseball bat. And I've yet to see the young lady who can dance the role of the Sugar Plum Fairy in the Nutcracker ballet, the first time she straps on pointe shoes.

The How-To-Do-Its

2. Skills take time.

You start out bad and you get better. There is no substitute for time in developing real skills. You can't acquire them in an instant. You can compress the time it takes with a concerted effort, but the time must still be invested if you are to succeed in your quest. Hence... 120 days at 30 minutes a day.

Good news and bad news about the how-to-do-its and skills.

The bad news is this... you can follow a procedure – a step-by-step description of a process – but that doesn't guarantee excellent, adequate, or even accurate implementation.

The good news is... even poor execution of the right what-to-dos and how-to-do-its will often result in a shockingly favorable outcome.

YOUR ACTION ITEMS...

☛ Read a book or listen to an audio program that is supposed to tell you "how-to" fix whatever it is you have identified as your Delta Initiative target.

☛ Evaluate the book or program for its "how-to" vs. its "what-to" value. If it really gives you the how-tos along with the what-tos, great! That means you should be able to take action, build skills and appropriately tackle your Delta Initiative target.

☛ If you find you really don't get the how-to-do-its along with the what-to-dos, then make a list of the knowledge and skills you think you'll have to acquire if you are going to change your Delta Initiative target.

TIP: There's magic in writing these things down. I recommend you <u>use the spreadsheet program I have provided</u> on the CD that came with this book.

△5△

U-NEED #3
THE RESOURCES TO GET IT DONE

"If you have always done it that way, it is probably wrong."

Charles Kittering

5

Nobody can do it all alone. You need resources. Tough to get everything you need from books, tapes and events.

Let me give you an example…

I recently moved into a brand new home. It is worth substantially more than what I paid for it, because I did some of the work myself.

But not all.

I had a general contractor who got the place from an empty lot to a near-finished product. I did the tile work, the painting, and the landscaping.

But I even had help on the parts I did myself. I got a master tile guy to work with me in the evenings. (His name is Kyle Barney. I call him Kyle, King of Tile, and if you need tile work in your house, this is the guy to call.) To be honest, I really helped him, not the other way around. Still, I estimate I saved 50% of what it would have taken to hire out the tile work in the conventional sense of the word.

For the paint, I bought a used paint sprayer. I made several trips to Home Depot and the paint store to get advice and direction on how to use it. (The nice thing about paint is, if you screw it up, you can just go over it again. It only took me one extra coat to get it right. I saved thousands.)

Landscaping, same thing. Lots of trips to Home Depot, questions to gardeners and sprinkler experts, landscape architects, even friends and neighbors with exceptional yards. The Soil Conservancy District in our area has a great demonstration garden and lots of information.

THE RESOURCES TO GET IT DONE

All of these were resources to "get it done."

For the last several months I've been finishing my basement myself. It was already framed and the rough electrical, plumbing and heating were already in. My sons and I have hung the drywall, driving every screw. We have done all the taping and mudding, all the finish electrical, including hanging ceiling fans and light fixtures. Again, all the paint and finished carpentry, most of the tile, most of the finished plumbing and most of the cabinetry have been or will be done by yours truly and sons.

But not all. There have been and are some things that I call in the experts for. Sometimes they work right along side me. Most of the time they explain what I need to do and then come back and check on my work.

But there is no way I could attack this project entirely on my own, without the help of experts. I have needed and continue to need RESOURCES to get the job done.

In building the house, the home improvement stores are great resources. So are the craftsmen who willingly share their advice or who work with me on a "scab" basis, saving me money, while picking up a few extra dollars for themselves.

In tackling just about anything from business challenges to personal and relationship issues, most of us need resources.

We may call on the resources to inform us. We may call on them to help us hone our skills. We may call on resources to actually do the work for us.

If you are going to produce an infomercial, odds are you'll be bringing in some help. You may write the script, but are you going to do the hosting, the camera work, the editing? Somebody has got to arrange for locations, testimonials, lighting and more. It's a complex thing and you can't go it alone.

And then there's the value of a third party perspective. You and your significant other may have a very clear picture of what's wrong with your relationship. Each of you may even have some pretty good ideas about how to fix it. But can the two of you agree, especially when emotions are running high? That "independent" third party -- a therapist or other detached person -- may prove invaluable in helping you get the job done.

The truth is, we like to be independent and self-reliant. And for the most part that's good. That sense of independence drives us to take care of our families, make a contribution to our communities, keeps us off of government hand-out programs and helps us appreciate and sacrifice for the principle of freedom.

But we cannot be wholly independent and achieve maximum success. We are social people. We are *interdependent*. And our society has been built on the principle of interdependence.

You have a job because your particular skill set is profitably useful to somebody else. You are a *resource* to your employer or your clients, customers, or patients. If you weren't, you wouldn't be of any use to anybody and you wouldn't have an income.

By the same token, you cannot rob others of the opportunity to be a resource to you.

Resources come in many forms. I've talked about books, audio programs, seminars and workshops. All of these are resources. Computers, machines and tools can be resources. Experts, advisors, craftsmen, can also be resources.

One of the most valuable resources you will ever encounter is a good **Coach**.
Think about it. The greatest athletes on the planet have coaches. Michael Jordan, Tiger Woods, Wayne Gretsky, Barry Bonds, Steve Young. They all had or have coaches. They are all athletically better than their coaches, but

The Resources To Get It Done

they have coaches nonetheless.

That's because they know the value of resources. As confident – even cocky – as the greatest athletes can be, they became as good as they are because they were *humble* enough to know they couldn't do it on their own.

On the other end of the spectrum, recovering alcoholics in the Alcoholics Anonymous program will be the first to admit that you can't do it alone. They build a support system that includes many people, but chief among them is their "sponsor" in the program.

That sponsor is the equivalent of a coach, and an invaluable resource.

Top athletes to alcoholics. They need help and guidance.

And so do you. If you're going to change what's sucking away at your life, you're going to need resources, and a good **Coach** is the best resource of all.

Today there are all kinds of coaches. Executive coaches, relationship coaches, personal coaches. The Delta Initiative formula was built on the model I developed in my primary role as a **Marketing Coach.**

If you want to change, get a coach.

Here are some suggestions for what to look for in your coach.

1. Get a coach who is somewhat removed from you personally. Family members may be qualified from a knowledge perspective, but the emotional attachments make it too difficult. They will either find it too hard to level with you and be firm when you are wavering, or you won't be able to force yourself to feel obliged to act on their coaching advice.

2. There are some circumstances where a

friend may be able to fill a coach role for you, but those instances are few and far between. The same reasons why family members can't be your coach hold with friends. They'll have a reluctance to hold your feet to the fire, and you'll have a reluctance to let them.

3. Business associates may be able to fill the bill, particularly if they are colleagues from outside of your company. These people won't be as affected by the "politics" of the office.

4. Your coaching relationship is generally a peer-to-peer relationship. You'll have a tough time working with someone who is not on your level from an education, occupation and socio-economic perspective. Of course, don't get carried away with this analysis. You don't have to see the prospective coach's college transcript. You simply have to feel like the two of you are on the same general level.

5. Find coaches who know what they're talking about. This is the place to check the background. I can help you *get more customers who will pay you more money, more often*™. I'm probably not the guy to help you quit smoking or fall back in love with your spouse.

6. Look for a coach with a critical eye and an ability to size up the situation. Michael Jordan, Tiger Woods, and Pete Sampras were all better players than their respective coaches. But all of their coaches had the knowledge and ability to spot flaws, prescribe the right fixes and "drill" their charges until those fixes had been installed.

7. Consider paying a professional coach. Money is glue. It's what makes both parties take it seriously. When you've got "skin in the game," you're more likely to do whatever it takes to get your money's worth. When a coach is being paid, he's more likely to do whatever it takes to be worth the money.

THE RESOURCES TO GET IT DONE

NOTE: As a general rule, the closer you are emotionally to your Coach, the more difficult the Coaching relationship is in the beginning. A spouse is deadly. A best friend can be a disaster. You are highly likely to develop a deep and close relationship with your Coach. But seldom is it best to start out that way.

Oh, and lest you think you'd never want to move into my house, with me having done so much of the work in the fully-finished basement, you might want to think again. It isn't perfect, but the general contractor who originally built the place confided to one his friends that I had done an awesome job!

YOUR ACTION ITEMS...

☛ Identify all the resources you're going to need in addressing your Delta Initiative target. Include informational, skill, and feedback resources, along with any execution help you will need to get the job done.

☛ Determine the criteria for a good coach to help you attack your Delta Initiative target. Think in terms of expertise, the ability to analyze the problem(s), the ability to organize, teach and lead.

☛ Create a short list of possible candidates. You may even conduct an informal interview with the candidates to determine their willingness and ability to perform in this critical capacity for you.

△ 6 △

U-NEED #4
FEEDBACK TO MAKE SURE YOU DO IT RIGHT

"It's not so much that we're afraid of change or so in love with the old ways, but it's that place in between that we fear... It's like being between trapezes. It's Linus when his blanket is in the dryer. There's nothing to hold on to."

Marilyn Ferguson

FEEDBACK TO MAKE SURE YOU DO IT RIGHT

6

One of the biggest reasons people don't take action following reading books, listening to tapes or attending events, is fear of failure; fear of doing it wrong. Feedback gives you the confidence to know you can do it right.

Let me share with you one of the most fascinating, if frustrating, experiences of my life.

Jay Abraham is one of the nation's most brilliant marketing advisors for small businesses. A few years ago, he conducted what he called, *The Ultimate Live Marketing Research Laboratory*. The program consisted of four, 2-day seminars, one every six months for two years. In between, the participants were to engage in a monthly peer coaching program. Three hundred entrepreneurs started the program, each having paid $5,000.00 to be part of the grand experiment. I was privileged to be asked by Jay to be one of the instructors.

My topic for the first seminar was how to create a Unique Selling Proposition, or what I call a **Unique Purchase Appeal**. I taught the principal and gave specific, step-by-step instruction as to the process of UPA development.

Six months later, at the second of the four events, I returned to teach another topic. When I took the stage to speak, I said, "Before I get started, I want to see how many of you did what I told you last time, and developed your Unique Purchase Appeal."

Now keep in mind that the original group of 300 had dwindled to about 280. Still, I was shocked and appalled to see only about 20

Feedback To Make Sure You Do It Right

hands go up in the room.

I asked those 20 to step to the microphone and recite for me their Unique Purchase Appeals. Of the 20, only three or four had something they were sure of, and that reflected having gone through the process I had taught.

Despite my shock and chagrin, I quickly came to realize I should have expected such an outcome. After all, if less than 10% of the books that get bought, actually get read, and if 93 out of 100 people reach retirement age financially unable to retire, and if 95% of all businesses fail in their first five years, isn't it a fairly logical conclusion that the implementation rate among seminar goers is between 1.4 and 8.4 percent?

I confess I *had* expected more, primarily because of the price people paid to be there. If you sink five grand into something like this, I reasoned, you will surely take action to insure the value of your investment.

Apparently not so. Apparently price has no bearing on follow-through.

So what does? Why don't people follow-through; take action; implement?

Laziness, lack of discipline, distractions. These are all reasons. And we'll address them when we get to accountability.

But one of the biggest action blockers is fear of failure.

I see this all the time in the marketing world. It's like a sub-conscious voice is talking to the business people I work with.

"Boy that's a good idea. I've got to put that one to work in my business.
"Now, how did Jim say to do that?
"But what if I do it wrong? What if I do it and it doesn't work?
"Well that'll mean I'm dumb; I'm a failure.
"Oh, I've never been good at this marketing

Feedback To Make Sure You Do It Right

stuff anyway."

The challenge with doing anything new is that we're almost bound to do it poorly at first. We have limited knowledge and virtually no skill. Yet somehow we expect ourselves to be perfect, right out of the blocks, and we stand ready to crucify ourselves when we're not.

Even more interesting is the form the crucifixion often takes.

Instead of actually blaming ourselves and our lack of knowledge and skill, we lay it at the feet of others. It's Jim's fault, or the media rep's. Or maybe you didn't get enough support from your spouse, or other people are too pressing on your time. Maybe you can't get "buy-in" from your team. Oh, and two of my favorites… "it's the economy," and "our whole industry is down."

The excuses abound, but one thing is certain. As long as you're laying it off on somebody or something else, you block your own ability to effect lasting, positive change.

You can avoid most of these problems with a little bit of feedback. I'm talking about regular and consistent feedback from advisors who know their stuff, are willing to tell the truth, and whom you respect and will listen to.

When seeking feedback, here's what to look for…

1. Look for feedback, not merely cheerleading. There are many who will tell you what you want to hear. And if your execution is good, you certainly want to know about it. But more important than the feel good stuff is the how to do it better stuff.

2. Make sure the feedback is specific. Again, generalities abound, but how does that help you fix it? My daughter was a professional ballerina. When she took her dance classes at all levels, she craved "corrections." Most

of the corrections she got were nuances… even minutia. But in her quest for perfection, she realized perfection is in the trifles. The same is true for most of the things we do.

3. Your quest may be for perfection, but you don't have to actually achieve it… nor should you necessarily expect to. And neither should your source of feedback expect perfection of you. The goal is progress. The progress may manifest itself in a big way, especially in the beginning. As your knowledge and skills increase, the progress may be more nuanced. By the same token, you may find that small changes yield huge results.

4. Don't take it personally. When you receive feedback that highlights your weaknesses and shortcomings, remember that you want the feedback. And remember the source of the feedback is on your side.

5. It is reasonable to expect your source of feedback to be courteous and sensitive in delivering the message (although it may not always be necessary). Still if a choice has to be made between a lack of courtesy and a lack of candor, opt for the candor and cowboy up.

6. Maintain the philosophy that anything worth doing is worth doing poorly, at first. Embrace the feedback for what it is… the gateway to increased knowledge and skill and the foundation of your ability to attack and ultimately conquer your Delta Initiative target.

7. Get enough of it. If you take a class once a week and have an instructor who gives you feedback on your efforts, you will improve and change at one level. If you take the class daily, your progress is likely to be dramatically faster.

8. Avoid feedback by committee. Too many

sources are too confusing. Everybody has an opinion and too often those opinions can be based on a lack of true knowledge. I hate it when a business person makes up an ad and shows it to everybody on his staff, including secretaries and mail room clerks, to get "feedback." There is a difference between feedback and opinion. You can get your feedback from a limited number of multiple sources, just make sure each source is qualified to give it.

To be sure, some things about your life will be easier to change than others. Some things are more important to change than others. You may find yourself resistant to some changes and particularly resistant to some feedback. Especially when the person providing it touches some of your emotional "hot buttons." Still, when it comes to changing anything in your life, consistent feedback is critical to your success.

No, you can't get it from books or audio

programs, and you can't get enough of it consistently enough from seminars and workshops. That's why the feedback part of the Delta Initiative formula is one of the more difficult elements to come by, and why it is so critically important to your success.

Remember, we're talking about a 30-minute a day, 120 day program of change here. Your source of feedback needs to be in it with you for the long haul.

YOUR ACTION ITEMS...

☞ You may have already identified a Coach or other source or sources of feedback in your resource assignment. If not, start this search now.

☞ Evaluate your own willingness and ability to listen to, accept and act on feedback. This can be a challenge to ego and emotions. Identify your "hot buttons" on paper, and prepare to put them on the back burner, so you will be open to the feedback you will receive as you work to change. Write down the strategies you will use to avoid negative reactions when your buttons are pushed in the feedback process.

∆ 7 ∆

U-NEED #5
ACCOUNTABILITY TO MAKE SURE YOU ACTUALLY DO IT

*"No person is your friend
who demands your silence, or
denies your right to grow."*

Alice Walker

Accountability To Make Sure You Actually Do It

7

Somebody has to hold your feet to the fire. Somebody has to consistently hold you accountable to make sure you do what you know you should, in a timely fashion.

They do exist, but there are precious few people in the world who are so self-motivated, so self-disciplined, that they can hold *themselves* accountable in virtually any and every aspect of their lives and thereby govern their own improvement.

Far more common, but still a relative rarity, are those who are so passionate about certain aspects of their lives that they immerse themselves in those aspects, chart the course for excellence and single-mindedly pursue it without the direction of others.

There are some things we're just naturally good at. Some things we enjoy and have worked at and in which we have developed significant skills. In these things, the work doesn't feel much like work. It's more like fun.

Unfortunately, and simultaneously fortunately, these are seldom the things that suck in our lives. These are the things that bring us happiness and joy. These are the things about our lives that bring satisfaction and contentment.

It is human nature to avoid and resist the things that suck. We don't want to deal with those things, no matter how much dealing with them is essential if we are to get rid of them and be happier with ourselves and our lives.

How then can you realistically expect to

Accountability To Make Sure You Actually Do It

govern, direct and hold yourself accountable in these areas? I won't kid *myself*. I can't. Don't kid *yourself*. You can't either.

The fact is, if you are to change, if you are to eliminate the suck factors in your life, you've got to surrender some control. You're going to have to relinquish some authority over yourself to somebody else.

There is precedent for this, you know. And interestingly enough, it comes from those who have achieved excellence in some aspect of their lives.

Tiger Woods exploded on the PGA tour, winning tournament after tournament including the Masters, his rookie year on the tour. But after skyrocketing to the top of the money-winner's chart, he made the decision to re-engineer his golf swing.

To do so, he worked with a Coach, to whom he gave a certain amount of authority over the source of his livelihood.

The cost to Tiger was significant. The effort to change the key elements of his swing took a few months. To perfect the changes took well over a year. And Tiger went through a long stretch where he didn't win much. Since then, however, he has re-emerged as the dominant player on the tour, with a swing that – while naturally will require continuous refinements and adjustments – should serve him at championship levels for decades to come.

Barry Bonds is not well liked by his teammates or by the press. By all reports, he is often surly and almost always self-centered. The man has flaws. There are things about Barry that suck, at least to the rest of us. But you gotta admit, the guy can hit a baseball. He can hit it a long way a lot of the time, and while it won't thrill me, as of this writing, there's a darn good chance Barry Bonds will become the greatest home run hitter of all time.

Accountability To Make Sure You Actually Do It

But early in his career, Barry was little more than an average hitter. He had power, but it took him eight years before he hit more than 40 home runs in one season. But, with all of his ego and self-absorption, at some point Barry had to be humble enough to say, "I want more out of my baseball career."

At that point of decision, he turned a portion of the control to coaches and advisors and allowed them to hold him accountable to change. He improved his game.

(Frankly, with all the allegations of steroid use, Barry may have wanted "more" badly enough to cheat.)

Still, the results speak for themselves. In 2001 he hit 73 home runs. Thirteen more than Babe Ruth , 12 more than Roger Maris, and three more than Mark McGwire slugged just three years earlier. Since then, nobody has come close, and with the crackdown on steroid use, most think nobody ever will.

Now, If Barry Bonds wants to change anything else in his life that sucks, he'll have to go through the same humble process. And so will I, and so will you.

Levels and intensity of accountability will vary with the Delta Initiative target to be attacked.

I have a son whose behavior, along with my inability to deal with it, landed him in a special program. His feedback and accountability was almost constant, 24/7 for 21 months.

My daughter danced up to six hours a day, six days a week on her way to becoming a professional ballerina, constantly surrendering accountability to her teachers and coaches.

There was a time when, to save my marriage, I had to make some changes. I visited with a counselor on a weekly basis for months.
Most of my clients work with me on a weekly basis to change the marketing systems of their

Accountability To Make Sure You Actually Do It

businesses and their own marketing habits and skills. Some only work with me every other week, a few multiple times a week.

In each of these cases, control had to be surrendered. Authority and even autonomy had to be relinquished to someone else, for a period of time.

My brother is a recovering alcoholic. He surrendered control 11 years ago now. The first thing Alcoholics Anonymous taught him was to surrender control to his "higher power;" to lose the "I can do this myself" attitude. He allowed others to hold him accountable on a daily basis for a time, then it went to several times a week, then several times a month, then monthly. Even now, after 11 years of sobriety, he still checks in with his AA group on a regular basis.

Are you willing… are you humble enough… to admit you can't eliminate the things that suck in your life without both feedback and accountability?

Can you hand some of the authority for holding you accountable over to somebody else for a season, subjecting yourself to a degree, to this person or group, for the sake of affecting a change in your life?

Note that you don't necessarily have to want to, you just have to be willing to, in spite of what you want.

My son didn't want to go into the program. We put him there.

My brother didn't want to admit he was an alcoholic. But ultimately he did.

I didn't want to admit I was failing as a husband and I certainly didn't want to "waste time" every week in the shrink's office. But I did it.

Whether to avoid even greater pain or to gain even better pleasure, those who manage to change do so by subordinating their

Accountability To Make Sure You Actually Do It

immediate wants and convenience for a greater long-term good. And they do it by allowing somebody else to hold them accountable.

Please understand that while you relinquish a certain amount of control for the sake of being held *accountable* to make the changes you say you want to make, you are not handing over one iota of *responsibility*.

If you fail, it will not be the fault of the coach or counselor or advisor or mentor or mastermind group, or whoever else you may have sought accountability to. They may hold you accountable, but you must hold yourself responsible.

At the end of the day, Tiger Woods, Barry Bonds, my son and daughter, my brother, my clients and me, were all responsible for the outcome.

These happen to be success stories. There are

many failures. Troubled men and women, criminals, drug addicts and alcoholics, even athletes with professional and perhaps all-star potential, that never make it. They may try for a time, but for whatever reason, they slip and never get up.

The causes are many, but in the end it comes down to this... They were unwilling or unable to hold themselves accountable to a person or a program, for a long enough period of time, to overcome their weaknesses and permanently install the required changes in their lives.

Bottom line. For the vast majority of us, change doesn't happen alone and it doesn't happen overnight. You're going to need help and you're going to need it for a while. At least for the next 120 days.

Don't like it? Tough. You've got a choice to make. Accept being held accountable by somebody else... or go back to watching the ballgame.

YOUR ACTION ITEMS...

☛ Evaluate on paper, your willingness to subject yourself to an outside authority. Are you willing to make commitments to somebody else at a frequency of daily to at least twice a month? Are you willing to report to that person, program or body, both your successes and your failures? Are you willing to do what that person, program or body tells you to do and accept both positive and negative feedback from that entity?

☛ Write down what it is worth to you to change. The chances are you're going to have to pay something for the accountability. And that's a good thing. We don't value what we don't pay for. And we also don't value what we pay little for. There is something to be said for having "skin in the game."

☛ If you're this far in the book and you

haven't returned to the ballgame, it's time to decide on the entity that will hold you accountable. Be it coach, counselor, advisor, mentor, group or program. It's time to narrow the search, thoroughly evaluate the candidates and make a decision. Use the recommendations in previous chapters as well as this one, to evaluate those candidates who can help you attack your Delta Initiative target.

▲ 8 ▲
YOUR BACKTIMED
30-MINUTE ACTION PLAN

"If you don't like the way the world is, you change it. You have an obligation to change it. You just do it one step at a time."

Marian Wright Edelman

YOUR BACKTIMED 30-MINUTE ACTION PLAN

8

Once all the ingredients are in place, how do you actually effect change in 120 days or less? How do you tackle any aspect of your life that currently sucks and has sucked -- perhaps your entire life long -- and change it? How do you set the wheels for permanent change in motion... in four months?

The answer is surprisingly simple.

You've heard the proverbial question, "How do you eat an elephant? One bite at a time." That's how you change your life.

Begin by determining your final outcome;

what you want life to be like once you've conquered your Delta Initiative target. You will be smoke free; you and your spouse will be madly in love again; your golf handicap will be reduced by seven strokes; your business revenues will be up 12% or more.

Second, determine how much time you are going to spend each day focusing and working on the Delta Initiative target to be changed. Minimum commitment is 30 minutes. You could go up to an hour or two.

NOTE: Don't get overzealous. If you say you're going to work on it for four hours a day, that's probably not realistic. You'll start out strong and burnout fast. It *is* realistic to go more than 30 minutes, but more than two hours is probably a pipe dream. This book, for example, was written in one-hour per day chunks.

By the same token, don't commit to 30 minutes a day and then decide you're going to save up your 30-minute segments until Friday, go for two and a half hours straight and figure you've met your commitment. You haven't. One of the biggest benefits of this process is forming the habit of consistent, manageable effort. There is magic in this. Don't blow it off. Thirty minutes a day means 30 minutes *every* day.

Yes, you can go past your 30 minutes (or hour or hour and a half) on occasion, but don't go too far past it. Stopping may be as important as starting, to develop in you the habit of self discipline.

If, on any given day you happen to go overboard by a significant time, do not assume that lets you off the hook for tomorrow's session. If you had budgeted 30 minutes on Monday and you go a full hour, you still have a 30 minute commitment Tuesday. You can't skip the next day.

And if you blow it one day and don't spend

any time on your commitment, you don't have to "make it up" the next day. You also don't give up on the whole project because you slip a few times. Just keep plugging away.

Even if you blow it for several days in a row, don't quit.

Remember, you don't have to *make* it up, you just can't *give* it up.

Next, break down and write down the outcomes into the specific milestones that must be achieved if you are going to accomplish the goal. If you're re-engineering the marketing systems of your business, one of your first milestones might be implementation of an upsell, add-on sell and cross-selling system. Another might be installation of a passive, incentive-based referral system.

Prioritize the milestones in order of importance and begin with the most important.

Your Backtimed 30-Minute Action Plan

Set a deadline, preferably no more than 30 days out, by which you want your milestone achieved.

Further break down your milestones into the major steps required to accomplish it.

(I'm sticking with a business example here because the milestones and tasks are easy to describe. The principle applies to anything.)

In the case of an up-sell, add-on and cross-selling system, there are five key steps or elements…

1. Pre-programmed offers
2. Scripts for your people to use in making the offers
3. Training for your people so they develop execution skills
4. Incentives for your people to get them using the system
5. A tracking system to make sure it's working and how well it's working

Break each major step down into the individual tasks that must be completed in order to accomplish the steps. Then determine how much time it will take to finish each of the individual tasks.

Finally "backtime" the effort you will put into each task, from your deadline date, to determine how many 30 minute segments it will take to get each task finished.

For example, if I were installing an up-sell, add-on, cross-selling system in retail business, I would say, "Okay, I need some companion product offers, some seasonal offers, some at-large offers and some counter offers. I think I can come up with a good collection of offers in three 30-minute sessions.

"I'll also need to come up with the signage and materials to support those offers, and that should take another three sessions.

"After that, my people will need scripts to

Your Backtimed 30-Minute Action Plan

guide them in presenting the offers, and knowing my writing skills, it should take about 5 sessions to complete those.

"I've then got to design my training process so my people are all on the same page and have the necessary knowledge and skills to present these offers. I think I can put that together in four sessions, and it'll take another two sessions to actually conduct the training with my staff.

"Oops, before I train them, though, I have to determine how I am going to entice them to operate the system until it becomes habit and part of our marketing culture around here. I should be able to figure out the incentive program in just one session.

"Finally, part of me says simply tracking my average sale should be enough to determine whether this effort is increasing it or not, but another part of me says I should be able to track the results in terms of percentage of customers taking us up on the up-sell offers and which staffers are succeeding with the program best. Hmmm. I think I'd better spend some time coming up with a reliable, simple-to-use tracking system. That'll probably take three or four sessions.

"And then I've got to arrange for printing of signage and materials and other logistical arrangements. I'm thinking a total of five sessions should cover all the coordination efforts."

All tolled, this project will take 23 sessions. When you take into consideration that you won't be working on the project on weekends, 23 working days equates to just about 30 calendar days to implement this system.

Once it's complete, backtime your next project and go through the same process again.

There is a case for 30-day action plans. A month is a good-sized bite. Almost everybody

Your Backtimed 30-Minute Action Plan

can deal with that. I am a big believer in annual marketing plans. I think marketing should be planned out for that long. But I also believe that executing in bites of 30 days at a time makes the big picture very manageable. It's not too much of the elephant, all in one sitting.

In 30-day chunks, the light is *always* at the end of the tunnel. Measurable progress can be seen, virtually on a daily basis. The "internal" feedback of seeing that progress is motivating. It helps keep you on track. And course adjustments along the way are easy to see and adapt to.

As you attack your Delta Initiative target, do so in action plans that are 30 days or less in length.

Your coach (or other advisor(s)) plays a vital role in the process in the following ways…

- You may need to consult with your coach to determine the specifics of your desired outcome.

- You may need to jointly decide on the milestones and the steps needed to accomplish each milestone.
- Your coach may be the source of the knowledge you need to acquire to achieve your objectives.
- Your coach will certainly be giving you feedback on the quantity and quality of your efforts.
- Your coach will certainly define, with you, the specific assignments you will complete within any given time frame and you will certainly report to your coach on a regular basis, whether you have completed the assignments or not.

As I coach businesses around the country, I have found that a weekly coaching conference is most effective, with the proviso, of course, that the client has the right, ability and responsibility to call on me, if needed, in the interim between regularly scheduled conference sessions.

Your Backtimed 30-Minute Action Plan

That's business coaching for relatively stable businesses. If a business is in immediate danger of failure, more frequent sessions may be required.

If a marriage is failing, daily coaching may be necessary. Same with drug, alcohol or smoking addictions. The point is this: You must determine, up front, the role your coach will play and at what frequency you will interact with your coach. You must also make that interaction a routine. Same time and duration. Same day or days of the week. Same interval between sessions.

The system works when you and your coach agree on the specific assignments you are to complete and the time by which they will be completed. And when you submit your assignments far enough in advance that your coach has time to carefully review your work, so you can get the benefit of his or her studied feedback.

Finally, it is best to provide yourself with incentives or rewards for accomplishing both your short and long-term objectives. These incentives vary greatly, of course, but the importance of rewards cannot be overstated. One of the great failings of many change efforts is failure to reward yourself for your mini-victories along the way. Build these incentives into your program in advance.

Something as simple as a 10-minute break can be a meaningful reward for finishing a single assignment. Candy bars, lunch out, going to a movie tonight, even watching the ballgame, can be nice incentives for getting all your assignments done in a day or a week, or just staying on task for your appointed 30 minutes or hour. Cash is good, so is travel or big entertainment events as you hit milestones or achieve your overall objective.

Oh, one other note. You need an off-season. Once you've conquered your first Delta Initiative target, take a break. In my

Your Backtimed 30-Minute Action Plan

experience as a business coach, I've seen that four to six months of this kind of intense effort is about all an individual can take without a break. Every sport has an off-season. You'll need one too. Take a couple of weeks off before you tackle your next initiative.

YOUR ACTION ITEMS...

Well what do you know... this whole chapter has been action items. But here are a few more...

1. Identify the best time of day for you to spend your 30 minutes on your Delta Initiative target. Maybe it's early in the morning right after your get up, or the first half hour of the work day. Perhaps it's on your lunch hour or just before you leave the office. Maybe after dinner or just before you go to bed. But now is the time to pick a time and stick to it. No cheating. STOP READING. Choose and write it down RIGHT NOW.

2. "Hire" your Coach.

3. Develop your first 30-day action plan.

4. Do it!

NOTE: Use the ACTION PLAN software provided on the CD that accompanies this book. It's just a simple spreadsheet planning document. But it's an easy way to complete all of the action items I've assigned to you, and to identify all the steps you'll be taking and skills you'll be installing on your way to conquering your Delta Initiative Target.

Δ CONCLUSION Δ
Gettin' Do IT

"The important thing is this: To be able at any moment to sacrifice what we are for what we could become."

Charles Dubois

Your Backtimed 30-Minute Action Plan

There is an old belief that you can make or break any habit in 30 days.

I'm not so sure I believe it. I've worked out for 30 days straight many times in my life, but today I don't. That habit never became fully integrated into my lifestyle.

Maybe it's because making a new, good habit usually also entails breaking one or more bad habits, and we only concentrate on one or the other for the 30 days.

Truth is, I don't know why it is, but I believe real, meaningful, permanent change takes time. I believe that for many things in our lives 120 days will do it. I believe that for many other things, the first 120 days are crucial. That is the time when you can learn what you need to learn and begin to develop the skills and habits you'll need. But the job may not be 100% complete in that time.

I know, for example, that one of the most dangerous things an alcoholic can ever think is "I've whipped this thing." For them, they remain "recovering" for the rest of their lives.

And isn't that the way it is for all of us? In so many aspects of our lives, don't we remain "recovering" forever?

It seems to me that one of the greatest secrets of our long-term success is to acknowledge that it may be temporary; that things can and probably will happen to derail us along the way.

We steel ourselves against those happenings

by learning what we need to do to succeed, developing the skills to execute the what-to-dos effectively, and relying on the strength of others for insight, help and feedback.

When we learn; when we know how to learn, develop habits and skills; and when we experience even small successes, the result is confidence in our ability to do whatever it takes to adapt, to change, to grow. That's a big part of what gives us the ability to achieve long-term success, regardless of short-term challenges.

And perhaps most importantly, we help assure our continued success by remaining humble enough to recognize our own weaknesses and be willing to turn the accountability over to someone else.

Ultimately, of course, we are all accountable to our Maker. He is our ultimate Coach. As we involve Him in our processes of change, we invoke unspeakable power in our quest.

Thirty minutes a day for 120 days. It's a good start; it's an easy process. You really can have the kind of life and business that you want, if you really want it.

So that's it. That's the Delta Initiative process. It's not quantum physics or brain-surgery. (Well, it is brain-surgery in a way, isn't it.) But it's not difficult or complicated.

I'm finished. And if this seems like an abrupt ending to you, good. That means I've done my job. It's time to stop reading and get going. It's time to DO something.

Now, if you'll excuse me, I'm going to install the habit of working out every day. And then I'm going to reward myself by watching a ballgame.

Δ Δ Δ

ABOUT THE AUTHOR

Jim Ackerman is a marketing consultant and developer of *The Principle Centered Marketing Coaching™ Program*, which is unparalleled for producing improved marketing results in small to mid-size businesses throughout North America. Participants in the Principle Centered Marketing Coaching Program implement -- and achieve satisfactory to exceptional outcomes -- at rates ranging from 63% to 93%, compared to 1.4 to 8.4 percent from other improvement programs.

Jim is founder of *The Marketing Wizards Alliance™* and author of *The Marketing Wizards Alliance Newsletter*, offering an in-depth look at a marketing principle, strategy or tactic every month.

Jim is also a national columnist and a renowned speaker. As a member of the National Speakers Association, Jim addresses audiences for companies and associations across the globe, always helping his audiences *Get More Customers Who Will Pay You More Money, More Often™* , and now, helping them engineer positive change in their organizations, through the Delta Initiative process.

Put THE DELTA INITIATIVE to Work in Your Business

Jim Ackerman can help you *Get More Customers Who Will Pay You More Money, More Often*™ the fastest, easiest, most cost-effective ways possible.

Employ his Delta Initiative Process through his Principle-Centered Marketing Coaching™ Program, or have him speak at your next company or association meeting.

Contact Jim at Ascend Marketing, Inc.
800.584.7585
or at mail@ascendmarketing.com.

As a Delta Initiative reader Jim will provide you with a FREE Marketing Fitness Check-up (A $147.00 value), when you request information about the Coaching Program, or about his speaking services.

For business or personal changes inquire about Jim's CHANGINEERING™ program.

For Additional Copies of
THE DELTA INITIATIVE
Call 800.584.7585 or visit
www.thedeltainitiative.com
www.ascendmarketing.com
www.jimackermanspeaks.com

THE DELTA INITIATIVE

Some of Jim Ackerman's Additional Work...

Books

How To Get More Customers Who Will Pay You More Money, More Often™ (Ascend)

Mission Possible Volume I (Insight Publishing)

Slaying Goliath (Ascend -- Due out in 2006)

Audio Programs

How To Get More Customers Who Will Pay You More Money, More Often™

The 4 Essential Marketing Secrets That Guarantee You'll Never Worry About Lousy Sales Again

Retailer Assault Vehicle... 12 Essential Marketing Principles, Strategies & Tactics to Help Retailers "Get More Customers Who Will Pay You More Money, More Often™

Marketing Gems... How To Quickly Get More Customers Who Will Pay You More Money, More Often™ in the Jewelry Business

Master Marketing...For Plumbing, HVAC & Electrical Contractors

For a more comprehensive listing or to order, call the toll free number or visit the websites on the previous page.